Media Genius

CREATE YOUR OWN

FILM OR TV SHOW

Matt Anniss

raintree
a Capstone company — publishers for children

Raintree is an imprint of Capstone Global Library Limited, a company incorporated in England and Wales having its registered office at 264 Banbury Road, Oxford, OX2 7DY – Registered company number: 6695582

www.raintree.co.uk
myorders@raintree.co.uk

Edited by James Benefield and Helen Cox Cannons
Designed by Steve Mead
Original illustrations © Capstone Global Library Ltd 2016
Picture research by Morgan Walters
Production by Victoria Fitzgerald
Originated by Capstone Global Library Ltd
Printed and bound in China

ISBN 978 1 474 71374 0
20 19 18 17 16
10 9 8 7 6 5 4 3 2 1

British Library Cataloguing in Publication Data
A full catalogue record for this book is available from the British Library.

Acknowledgements
We would like to thank the following for permission to reproduce photographs: Alamy: Image Source Plus, 12; Corbis: 2/Ocean, cover, 42, Frederic Soltan, 36, Louie Psihoyos, 35, TWPhoto, 30; Getty Images: Hill Street Studios, 18, James Devaney, 43, Leon Bennett, 17, Matt Carr, 41, Matthew Horwood, 10, Peter Bischoff, 4, Pool APESTEGUY/SIMON, 31, Rachel Murray, 5, Syfy, 21, Thinkstock Images, 23; iStockphoto:lovleah, 26, Pamela Moore, 39; Newscom: Dave Penman/REX, 9; Shutterstock: Alexandru Nika, 7, Alexey Boldin, (phone) top 25, ChameleonsEye, 20, Christian Bertrand, 29, cobalt88, (TV) 8, (tablet) middle 25, Denis Dryashkin, 37, Goodluz, 40, Gorosi, 6, keellla, (video camera) bottom 25, Kzenon, 28, Margarita Vodopyanova, 24, MaxyM, 19, Monkey Business Images, 32, Nenov Brothers Images, (webcam) middle 25, PAN Photo Agency, 38, Rashevskyi Viacheslav, bottom 13, Salim October, (reporter) 8, Samo Trebizan, 34, Samuel Borges Photography, top 13, Sergey Novikov, 33, Syda Productions, 16, Tom Wang, 22, Zurijeta, 14

We would like to thank Nicola Armitage for her invaluable help in the preparation of this book.

Contents

INTRODUCTION

Do it yourself!

Do you dream of being the next Steven Spielberg or David Attenborough? Do you have a desire to make people laugh, cry or think deeply? Or perhaps you'd like to tell a great story, or present surprising or little-known facts in an entertaining way? If your answer is "yes" to any of those questions, you may want to consider making your own films and TV shows! It would have once been beyond the means of most young people to make a film or TV programme. Filmmaking is now accessible to almost anyone, thanks to modern technology.

Lots of people, money and equipment are needed to make Hollywood blockbusters. However, you can also get great results with just a few friends and your smartphone!

Between 2009 and 2014, six American teenagers ran their own TV channel on YouTube called Our2ndLife. It turned them into worldwide stars, with nearly 3 million people tuning in to watch their weekly video updates. One member of the group, Trevor Moran, posted his first clip on YouTube when he was just 10 years old!

Quick and easy

Filmmaking is an easy hobby to start – you may already have some of the equipment at your disposal! For example, if you have access to a webcam, smartphone, digital camera or tablet computer, then you're pretty much ready to start. Once you've read this book, you'll know just how easy it is to film something cool and edit it into an amazing video on your computer. You're then ready to share your film, if you want to.

Many filmmakers start out this way. Today, an increasing number of people working in the film and TV industry got their big break after sharing home movies online. There are many websites you can use to share things you film, but one of the most popular is YouTube.

CHAPTER 1

Choosing your style

It's useful to take some time to think about the style of film or TV show you'd like to make. For example, you need to choose between fact and fiction.

Spend an afternoon flicking between TV channels and you'll see just how many different types of films and shows you could make.

Separating fact from fiction

Factual films and TV shows are about real things, people, places and events. This is sometimes called non-fiction. Everything else is classed as fiction. By and large, fictional works are created purely for entertainment. Fiction contains stories, characters and situations thought up by a writer.

Factual films and shows can also be entertaining. However, the main reason factual shows and films are created is to be informative. They might explain how animals live their lives, why historical events took place or what's happening in the world.

Are you struggling to choose between these two styles of filmmaking? The following multiple-choice quiz could help.

FACT or FICTION?

Which of the following most appeals to you?
A: Learning new things
B: Writing stories

Which of the following do you most enjoy?
A: Meeting new people and hearing their stories
B: Making my friends laugh

Which of the following would you most like to film?
A: Interesting things happening in my neighbourhood
B: People in costumes acting out stories

What would be your ideal role in a film or TV show?
A: I'd like to film, direct and interview people on camera
B: I'd like to direct and perform

If you answered mostly…
A: You're a born factual filmmaker
B: You should concentrate on fictional films and TV shows

That's a fact!

Deciding between focusing on fact or fiction is merely the beginning of your filmmaking journey. Next, you need to decide on the style of film or show you wish to make.

Different styles are sometimes called genres. Grouping films and TV shows by their genres helps people know what to expect. Popular factual genres include:

CURRENT AFFAIRS

Current affairs programmes focus on contemporary events. Content includes news reports and investigations into issues that affect our day-to-day lives. They're based on facts and include interviews with people close to the story.

DOCUMENTARIES

Documentaries explore an interesting subject in greater depth. Documentaries often use a combination of interviews and film footage. Some of the most popular ones focus on the natural world. Great examples include *March of the Penguins* and *The Crimson Wing*.

DOCU-DRAMA

Docu-dramas blur the boundaries between fact and fiction, by getting actors to recreate real events. Docu-dramas often focus on events from history or amazing real-life stories.

Television news is the world's most popular style of factual programming. However, there are many other options for would-be factual filmmakers.

Some of the most popular TV series are those that focus on the world around us, such as *Africa*, *Frozen Planet*, and *Secret Life of Birds*, all presented by David Attenborough. However, filming animals in the wild can be difficult and dangerous, so should only be done by trained professionals.

The long or short of it

Factual films and programmes can be as simple or complicated as you wish. For example, it wouldn't take you long to make a short news report about your school football team. However, filming a documentary about the history of football would take much longer.

Success Story

According to the Guinness World Records, the world's most popular factual TV series is *Top Gear*. This British show about cars has been shown in 212 different countries worldwide!

In fictional film and TV genres, you can let your imagination run wild – just like the creators of *Doctor Who* do. There's almost no limit to the weird and wonderful things that you can come up with.

Use your imagination!

If you had to list your favourite films and TV programmes, how many would be works of fiction? Unless you only watch documentaries and news programmes, most of what you watch is probably going to be fiction. So what sort of fictional shows and programmes do you enjoy the most?

When it comes to fiction, there are many genres for budding filmmakers to choose from. Comedies make us laugh and dramas tell gripping stories about believable characters in real-world situations. Also popular is science fiction (sometimes shortened to sci-fi), which is all about possible future worlds.

Styles within styles

Many of these film and TV genres have their own sub-genres. These are like styles within a style. Below are a few genres and some of the sub-genres associated with them. How many more can you think of?

DRAMA
Cop show
Gangster film
Medical drama
Soap opera
Thriller
Film noir

COMEDY
Stand-up comedy
Sketch comedy
Sitcom
Cartoon
Romantic comedy
Buddy movie

SCI-FI
Time travel
Superheroes
Space travel
Horror

ENTERTAINMENT
Quiz show
Talk show
Variety show
Reality television

No limits!

These genres, sub-genres and formats are merely a guide. Many of the best films and TV shows bend these rules, either by combining two or more styles or even creating a new sub-genre of their own. There's no limit to what you can do – let your imagination run free and see what you can come up with!

Start small or aim high?

When deciding whether to make a film or a TV show, ask yourself this: Do you want to work alone, with a small group of friends or involve lots of people? The more complicated and ambitious your project, the more help you'll need. For example, you could make a one-off documentary TV programme by yourself. You'll just need to do all the filming and interview all the people. Making stuff gets more complicated if you want to tell a story over the course of a film or several episodes of a TV series. You'll need people to act, look after costumes, help you film and more.

You might dream of making an epic film, but starting with a short TV show on your own may be easier.

The way people watch films and TV shows is changing. Many people now choose to watch their entertainment online. Every month, more than a billion people watch videos on YouTube, the world's most popular video-sharing website. According to experts, videos stand a greater chance of attracting viewers if they're relatively short. The average length of the 100 most popular YouTube clips is just 5 minutes.

Money matters

Then there's the matter of cost. According to film industry research, average production costs of a Hollywood film in 2013 were an astonishing $71 million (£46.7 million). Not all successful films cost this much to make, of course. The 2004 film *My Big Fat Greek Wedding* cost an estimated $5 million (£3 million) to make, but earned over $370 million (£243 million) in total worldwide.

Most filmmakers don't have heaps of cash, however. And you can make fun films and TV shows with little or no budget – just the cost of a smartphone and any editing technology that you may want to buy. You can save costs by borrowing equipment. You can also ask friends to film and act for free.

CHAPTER 2

Planning your FILM or TV SHOW

Now you have an idea of the kind of film or TV programme you'd like to make. The next step is to work out how you're going to make it. There are many things you'll need to think about, including:

- How long is the film or TV programme going to be?
- Will it be a one-off programme or film, or will it be split into a number of different episodes?
- What equipment will I need and where will I film?
- Who will it feature?

You're probably keen to get that camera in your hands. However, before you get started, you will need to do some careful planning.

Work it out

Working out a rough structure is a good place to start. How do you want your film or TV programme to begin and end? Once you know this, you can flesh out the story in between.

THE KNOWLEDGE

Many films and TV shows use a blueprint known as the Three-Act Structure. Think of it as a line with a beginning, middle and end. The first and final acts are usually of a similar length, with the middle act being a little longer.

Act 1
This introduces the characters and sets up the story. Towards the end of the act, there will be a plot point – a major twist in the story to keep viewers interested.

Act 2
This is the middle section of the film or show. It usually includes a twist called the midpoint roughly halfway through. There is usually a second plot point at the end.

Act 3
This is the conclusion of the story, or climax. It wraps up the plot with the story's characters somehow changed.

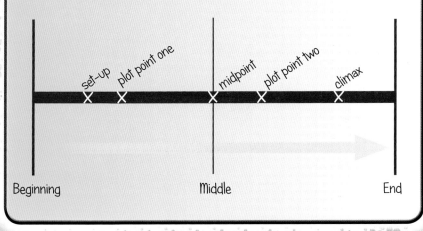

set-up plot point one midpoint plot point two climax

Beginning   Middle   End

Research and planning

The best factual films and shows, particularly documentaries, have two key elements:

WELL-RESEARCHED FACTS

These can be taken from books, newspapers, TV news reports and websites. Some sources are more reliable than others. For example, an article in a professional scientific magazine detailing a new piece of research would be considered reliable. However, a personal blog or wiki site may not be. Never assume that what you read has been fact-checked, especially if it's a personal blog post or web article. Where possible, it's worth finding two or three sources for a fact before including it in your film.

INTERVIEWS

These are usually with people who are relevant to the story. They could be witnesses to an event or experts in the subject you're covering. If you're planning on interviewing people, find out as much as you can about the people beforehand. This helps you to prepare meaningful and appropriate questions you can ask during the interview.

If you're planning on making a documentary, you need to find out as much as you can about your subject matter. Try starting your research by reading books or searching the internet.

Finding the right balance

Your documentary might be about a subject close to your heart or something that you feel passionate about. Even so, the best documentaries offer balanced viewpoints. That means selecting facts that show both sides of the story, as well as interviewees with differing opinions. You can always conclude by agreeing with one side of the argument, but overall your film should be even-handed.

Success Story

Trace Gaynor (right) and Stephen Sotor were just 11 years old when they made their first documentary film. Their 2004 film *Tween's Life* featured interviews with their friends. Two years later, their second film, *Genie In A Bottle: Unleashed*, was shown at film festivals around the world.

Scriptwriting

Whether you plan to tell a true story or one you've made up, you'll need to write a script. If you are making fiction, this contains the words you'd like your characters to say. If you're making a documentary, a script will contain what will be said between interview clips. For both types of film, there will be lots of other important information. The following script excerpt contains some examples of what is in a script.

A script is an important document containing instructions. Scripts should include information about the location of the scene, the time of day, the words you'd like the actors to say and movements you'd like them to make.

SCENE 1

TOM'S BEDROOM – DAY

TOM and JULIE stand by the window. TOM looks sad.

TOM
(Sighing)
I'm not sure this rain will ever end.

JULIE
The storm will pass eventually.

JULIE turns towards TOM.

What are you really thinking about?

TOM looks at JULIE, then down at the floor.

TOM
I guess I just miss Rex. He always loved playing in the rain.

JULIE hugs TOM.

JULIE
Do you remember that time he chased his own tail for half an hour?

TOM
(Smiling)
Yeah, that was funny. He was a great dog, but really stupid!

Cast and crew

Visit any major film set and you'll see dozens of people buzzing around. Each person has a part to play in the production process. Some of the more common roles in film and TV production include:

DIRECTOR
This person calls the shots by giving instructions to actors and camera operators.

PRODUCER
This person oversees the running of the entire project, leaving the director to concentrate on filming.

CINEMATOGRAPHER
He or she controls the style and look of the film, usually by changing the lighting or by picking out different types of camera lenses to use. This person works closely with a lighting crew.

CAMERA OPERATORS
They film the action. Many films and TV programmes have lots of cameras and operators to film scenes from different angles.

SOUND RECORDISTS
These people get sound recordings of the actors during filming. They may work with teams of technicians.

MAKE-UP ARTIST
This person makes sure the actors and extras look like the characters they're portraying on-screen.

ACTORS (THE CAST)
These are people who play the characters you've created.

EXTRAS
Sometimes called "background actors", these people don't speak and are there to supplement the main characters, for example in crowd scenes.

A director at work

This make-up artist is helping someone to get into character.

A little help from your friends

Try getting your classmates involved in your film. They might have some great ideas, a burning desire to act or even want to lend a hand with making costumes! If you're making a documentary, they could help with research, find people to interview or even operate the camera.

STAY SAFE

When using the internet, always get a parent, teacher or other responsible adult to help you out. Remember not to talk to strangers on chat services, however friendly they may seem.

Once you've found people for your film's cast and crew, you need to think about filming locations. Your school may let you use the building for filming after hours or at weekends.

Location, location, location

So, where are you going to film your first masterpiece? You may need to find several different locations depending on what your film or TV programme is about. You'll need places to set a fictional story or to film footage for a documentary.

Pro Tip

If the making of your film or show involves filming members of the public, you need to get permission. This is known in the world of TV and films as consent. You'll need to ask anyone being filmed, and those who own the locations you use, to sign a consent form. You can find templates for these consent forms online, but run these by an adult before you get them signed.

Get thinking!

You may need to be imaginative with your choices for filming locations. For example, it may be possible to film at school as long as you get permission. Also, local places of worship and community centres often have rooms you can hire for a small fee. Parks, friends' homes, playing fields and the street where you live can also be useful free locations.

Your own home might seem like a boring choice, but with a bit of effort you can change its appearance to fit the film. You could move furniture around, put up pictures or posters, or even use props. Objects such as drinking glasses, walking sticks, pens, bottles, books and DVD cases can help your sets look real.

It's important that the costumes you choose reflect what's happening in the film. For example, If the story is supposed to take place in winter, it would be inappropriate for an actress to be wearing a summer holiday outfit like the one below!

PRODUCTION
DIRECTOR
CAMERA
DATE   SCENE   TAKE

Preparing to shoot

If everything has gone to plan, you should almost be ready to start filming, or shooting. Before you start, there are still a couple of pieces of the filmmaking jigsaw puzzle missing.

Shot list

This is a scene-by-scene breakdown, in the form of a list, of everything a director wants to film. The shot list can be used to keep track of what a director needs to film as he or she goes along, even if he or she is making a documentary.

Unusual camera movements and shots make your film interesting. You don't need expensive equipment. Try mounting your camera on a skateboard for a moving shot. Or how about seeing the inside of a drawer as a character opens it? The shot list for the beginning of a scene may start as follows:

1. A shot to show the location and situation. This is called an establishing shot.
2. A long shot showing the main character in the distance.
3. A tracking shot following that character walking through a scene.
4. A medium shot of two characters meeting, possibly from the waist up.
5. A close-up of the two characters talking.

Storyboard

A storyboard is a step-by-step guide to how you want each scene to look. It looks a little like a comic strip. It can be used to help decide the kind of shots and camera angles you'd like to use in each scene.

In animation, animators often follow a storyboard (like this one) and a shot list combined. This helps them to explain what they need to animate in great detail.

Getting your hands on hardware

The final step of the planning process is an important one: getting hold of your filming equipment. There are a number of options, each with their own advantages and disadvantages. If you are having trouble finding any of it, research to see if there are filmmaking groups for young people in your area who can lend you their equipment.

Pro Tip

Smartphone

ADVANTAGES
- Easy to use
- Excellent for filming quickly

DISADVANTAGES
- Can only store small amounts of footage
- Poor picture quality
- Hard to hold still

Tablet computer

ADVANTAGES
- Excellent for filming quickly
- Large screen to play back footage

DISADVANTAGES
- Can only store small amounts of footage
- Poor picture quality

Webcam

ADVANTAGES
- Stores film footage on a computer

DISADVANTAGES
- Needs to be connected to a computer
- Poor picture quality

Video camera/Camcorder

ADVANTAGES
- Great picture quality
- Designed for filmmaking
- More features that can be used during filming

DISADVANTAGES
- Can be expensive to buy

CHAPTER 3

Filming your
FILM or SHOW
TV

You are now ready to make films! Remember that filming can be time-consuming and stressful, but it will all be worth it when you see the finished results!

After all that planning, you should now be ready and raring to go. On the first day of filming, you're likely to experience a mixture of feelings – excitement, nervousness, even a little stress as you remember all the things you need to do. This is natural. Just take your time and try to enjoy it.

No need to rush

Making films and TV shows is a time-consuming process, so you'll need to be patient. Allow enough time for everything, as things can go wrong. For example, actors might forget their lines, or you may want to film a number of different versions of the same scene (known as takes) to try different things out.

It might also be tricky to get the answers you're looking for from interviewees, or something might go wrong with the equipment. You also need to allow time for people to change costumes, move between locations and set up equipment. Filming a scene may only take a few minutes, but setting up the next scene might take three or four times as long!

Last-minute checks

Before you head to the set, or shoot, why not make a checklist to make sure you're fully prepared? The following list might be a good start:

- Copies of the script for every member of the cast and crew
- Shot list
- Camcorder/smartphone/tablet/webcam/microphones and other filming equipment
- Consent forms
- Addresses of filming locations
- Names of actors or interviewees
- Costumes and props

Lights, camera, action!

Depending on the type of film or show you're filming, there are different ways of conducting a shoot. It's worth familiarizing yourself with the process before you start, especially if you have not done it before. There are no set rules, though – if you have ideas you'd like to try out, just go for it!

Filming fiction

Traditionally, works of fiction are filmed by following the script, storyboard and shot list. That means filming a number of takes of the same scene, often from different angles, until you're happy with the results. Once you've done that, you can move on to the next scene. Don't worry about recording more footage than you need – you can select the best bits to use later.

Don't just rely on the script to tell a story. You could use a montage which shows the passing of time. For example, if you are shooting a runner training for a race, you could use a mix of shots over several days to background music. Also, don't forget continuity. This means making sure everything on the camera looks the same from shot to shot, from hairstyles to lighting.

If you're filming interviews, listen to the interviewees' answers. Don't be afraid to ask questions based on what they say, as well as those you've prepared beforehand.

Filming footage of athletes in action from different angles could help make your sports documentary sparkle. You could even get the athletes themselves to talk over the action afterwards. This is known in the business as a "voiceover".

Factual filming

The process for filming documentaries does not always follow a set order. You can film the elements needed in any order you wish, recording interviews and additional footage as you go along. For example, if the documentary is about sport, you may want to film athletes training or competing. Also, if you find out something unexpected on the way, you may want to go back and interview somebody again. This additional footage is important, as it helps make the documentary interesting. You can edit it all in order later.

THE KNOWLEDGE

While some films (and some TV shows) are still shot on photographic film, much recording is now done digitally. This means filming something on a digital camera, camcorder, smartphone or tablet. Here, the recording is saved inside the device as computer data. The storage capacity of devices varies, so you may have to stop recording and transfer data to a computer or hard drive if you run out of space.

CHAPTER 4

Finishing your
FILM or TV SHOW

Finished films are the result of a long period after shooting has finished, known as post-production. This part of filmmaking can sometimes take longer than the filming. During post-production, you have to select and sequence (known as editing) the best bits of footage, and then add any extra touches, such as music and special effects.

Following filming, the time-consuming task of editing begins. This is the process of turning the raw footage you've filmed into a masterpiece!

THE KNOWLEDGE

In the film and TV production industry, a person responsible for editing is known as an editor. They're a trained specialist with a talent for selecting and joining together the best bits of footage, usually under the supervision of the director.

Rough cut

The editing process can be quite time-consuming, as it involves trawling through a lot of raw film footage. It can take a skilled editor around three months to produce the first edit of a professional feature film, known as the rough cut. Finishing the final cut might take another month.

The terms "rough cut" and "final cut" refer to the traditional process of physically cutting up and ordering photographic film. Today, most editing is done on computers, using special editing software.

Editing software is available for smartphones and tablets, but most film editing is done on laptops or desktop computers. To use this method, you'll need to transfer the footage from the camera, phone or tablet to a computer. This is normally very simple to do. It involves connecting the camera to the computer using a USB lead, then dragging the film files to your computer's hard drive.

Final cut

To edit your film, you'll need editing software. Luckily, there are loads of free programs out there. Most PCs now come with Windows Movie Maker installed. If not, it can be downloaded from the Microsoft website for free. Some Apple devices come bundled with iMovie, which can also be bought cheaply from the App Store. If these don't suit your needs, there are plenty of other free editing software packages available. If it's not your personal computer, remember to ask permission before downloading software.

Useful tools

Every editing program is slightly different, but they all offer similar features. They all allow you to load up film footage, select the parts you want to use, and then arrange them on-screen using a drag-and-drop system. You can shorten longer footage, stitch together different takes and add effects.

Pro Tip

If you want to finish your film quickly, there are smartphone apps and websites that will help by doing it for you. A good example is Magisto, which edits together cool-looking videos using clips you've selected. While great for making films quickly, these apps don't give you much control over the editing process.

If you know someone with experience of editing film clips, why not get them to help you create your "final cut"? You can still call the shots, just like a professional film director!

Editing software for beginners

Menu
This is where you'll find all the key controls for editing your film, such as copy, cut and paste, plus other useful tools.

Contents
Drag film clips you'd like to use here, before putting them into your film timeline.

FILE   EDIT   VIEW

Import

Export

Edit

Video 1

Timeline
This is where you arrange the clips that will make up your film. There is sometimes a clock here too, so you can see how long your film is.

Preview window
Watch individual clips or the entire contents of the timeline.

Finishing touches

By now, you might have got a rough cut of your film that you're happy with. If so, you might want to add a few extra touches to make it stand out. Many free or inexpensive editing software packages include special visual effects that can be used to spice up your film. Some programs also let you slow down or speed up footage, turn colour images into black-and-white images, or completely change the soundtrack.

Sounds alive

Adding music or sound effects is a great way to make your film even more memorable. For example, if you have made a film about ghosts, you could:

- use spooky theme music to set the scene and create a chilling mood
- add sound effects, such as doors creaking, to make certain moments of the film extra scary
- emphasize a big moment in the film by adding music that enhances what you're seeing on-screen.

You can record voiceovers for documentaries and news reports using a microphone, computer and voice recording software. This recording can then be dubbed onto the film during the editing process.

Foley artists make sound effects for films, often out of everyday objects. You could clip coconuts together to copy the sound of horses' hooves, or sprinkle rice onto a metal surface to create a sound like rain.

Pro Tip

Most music is copyright-protected, meaning you can't use it in films or TV shows without permission from the person who made it. Luckily, royalty-free music, which can be used without permission, also exists. You'll find this in online music libraries such as Freeplay Music and the YouTube Audio Library.

CHAPTER 5

Promoting your
FILM or TV SHOW

One day, posters for your films might be plastered across the side of a cinema. For now, you may have to settle for putting up home-made posters at school.

Once you've put the finishing touches on your first film or TV show, it's time to tell people about it. If you want people to see it, you'll need to turn it into a single video clip and save it, using a process called exporting. All editing software will let you export video. Then you'll need to develop a plan for showing people your work.

Promotion commotion

The process of raising awareness about a product or service is called marketing. Today, the success or failure of a film or TV series can come down to how well it's marketed to the public. According to a 2014 report in *Hollywood Reporter*, the average worldwide marketing spend on a big-budget film is a staggering $200 million (£133 million). Much of this money is spent on posters, and other advertisements on radio, television and the internet.

Get burning!

Clearly, you can't afford to spend much money on marketing your film, but there's plenty of less costly things you can do. Why not burn some DVDs for those who helped you make the film? It's good to get their feedback before you go public with the film.

Many laptops and desktop computers have the ability to "burn" DVDs. If yours does, you'll need to get hold of some DVD-R discs.

Pro Tip

Most filmmakers try to raise interest in their films by making trailers. These are short adverts featuring action from the film, with music and a voiceover explaining what the film is all about. Try to make your own trailer for your film.

In the showbiz industry, it's traditional to launch a new film by holding a glitzy premiere.

This is a test

Before a film's star-studded premiere, it'll have already been shown to small groups of people at events called test screenings. During these screenings, people working in the film industry or members of the public are asked to watch a film. They give feedback on the film by filling in a special questionnaire. These answers are mainly used to work out how to market a film, but sometimes they're even used to change the film. Some big-budget films can face reshoots.

The big premiere

When you're ready to launch your first big- or small-screen masterpiece, you could hold your own premiere. Invite your friends, family and those who've helped you out to a special screening at home, school or a local community centre. You could even have a question-and-answer session at the end, where you talk about the making of the film.

Make your own film questionnaire

Try to hold your own test screening for friends, complete with questionnaires based on those used by film studios! Here are a few questions to get you going, but feel free to think of your own:

did you think of the film overall?

Which characters/ scenes did you like/ dislike the most?

Would you recommend this film to your friends?

What could we do to improve the film?

What did you think of the ending?

If your film or TV show gets an excited response, you know you're on the right track! If not, ask those who've seen it to provide detailed, honest feedback about where and how you could improve it.

Today, more people than ever before watch films and TV shows online.

Sharing it with the world

The internet is great for budding filmmakers. It allows them to get their work into the public domain without the need to rely on expensive marketing tricks, such as advertising campaigns. You could upload your film or TV show to video-sharing sites such as YouTube and Vimeo. Remember though, if you're under 13 years of age, get a responsible adult to do it for you.

The hard sell

Thousands of video clips are uploaded to sharing sites every minute, so you'll still have to work hard on promotion if you want your project to go viral. This is an expression used when something spreads quickly on the internet. Getting a video to go viral is no easy task, but the following will give you a much greater chance of success:

- Keep your video clip short.
- Inspire your audience, for example with amazing real-life stories.
- Be upbeat, funny or include content likely to stir emotions.
- Link your video clip to current events or subjects that people are talking about online.

Success Story

Another great way to spread the word is to create your own YouTube channel. This allows you to post a number of video clips to one page, which viewers can subscribe to. This is what filmmaker Ari Gold did to promote his 2008 film *Adventures of Power*. He posted more than 70 video clips to his channel, including footage not shown in the film. His channel received more than 200,000 views and around 1,000 subscribers, and increased sales of DVDs.

Although he won a Student Oscar for his short film *Helicopter*, Ari Gold still found it hard to raise interest in his feature-length comedy flick *Adventures of Power*. For this reason, he turned to YouTube to help spread the word.

Just the beginning!

How have you found your filmmaking adventure? If all has gone to plan, your head should already be full of ideas. You might be thinking about things you can do to promote your project and other films and shows you can make in the future.

Once you've got the filmmaking bug, you'll be hooked for life. Many film directors began by making home movies during their teenage years.

Success Story

Steven Spielberg, one of the most successful directors of all time, began by making home movies as a teenager. He quickly found work in the industry, directing his first TV film at the age of 24. He was only 28 when the film *Jaws* was released, one of the biggest blockbusters of all time!

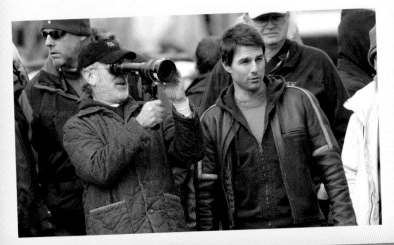

There's no limit!

The great thing about filmmaking is that the only limit is your imagination. The world is full of interesting subjects to investigate, stories to tell and events to film. Every time you set out to make a new film or TV show, the process will be a little bit easier. There will be gradual improvements in your scriptwriting, directing, filming and editing skills.

You'll soon be finding all sorts of excuses to pursue your hobby. For example, if you have a school history project to do, you could film a recreation of the events being discussed in class. You could make a video explaining how DNA works for a science project.

Career move

There is no limit to what you can do with filmmaking. If you're lucky, it could even lead to a career in the film and TV industry. You might not be the director of a big-budget Hollywood smash hit yet, but you can still wow people with brilliantly crafted documentaries, comedy sketch shows or home-made TV dramas. Think big! And good luck!

Glossary

blockbuster hugely successful and popular film, often one that also cost a great deal to make

campaign planned sequence of events used to achieve a goal, for example raising awareness of the release of a new film through advertising and marketing

contemporary something happening right now, in the present time

continuity process of ensuring everything appearing "on camera" looks the same from shot to shot, from hairstyles to lighting

dubbing process of adding sounds (music, speaking or effects) to a film or television show

film noir style of crime film renowned for the use of shady characters and minimal use of lighting. *Noir* means "black" in French.

foley artist person who specializes in making and recording special effects for films and TV programmes

gangster film type of crime film that focuses on criminal gangs and their activities

genre style or category of film, for example thriller, comedy or documentary

home movie film made for personal use without special equipment, for example a film of a person's holiday

interviewee person who is being interviewed by someone

marketing process of raising awareness of a product or service in order to attract more customers or viewers

montage series of shots to show something happening over time

premiere first time a film or television show is shown, either to the public or an invited audience of special guests

prop object the actors use on camera, in a film or TV programme

public domain content that is available to the public to legally use for free

reshoot when a cast and crew go back and film scenes, or parts of scenes, again after they think they have finished filming everything. This is usually based on feedback from a test screening.

romantic comedy (rom-com) style of funny film based on love and relationships

set up arrange the position of cameras, scenery and other equipment on a film or TV shoot

soundtrack sound that accompanies the pictures on a film or TV show, which can include speech, music and effects

sub-genre small category of film within a larger category. For example, a gangster film would be in the larger category of crime films.

test screening when members of the public and the film industry are invited to watch and comment on a film. Their comments can cause a film to have reshoots or re-editing.

thriller type of film or TV series known for being particularly exciting or gripping

voiceover voice in a film or television show, of a person who is heard but not seen, or not seen talking

Find out more

Books

Andrew Jenks: My Adventures as a Young Filmmaker, Andrew Jenks (Scholastic Press, 2013)

How to Make a Movie in 10 Easy Lessons (Super Skills), Robert Blofield (Walter Foster Jr., 2015)

Kids Guide to Movie Making, Shelley Frost (CreativeSpace Independent Publishing, 2011)

Movie Maker: The Ultimate Guide to Making Films, Tim Grabham, Suridh Hassan, Dave Reeve, Clare Richards, Garry Parsons (Candlewick, 2010)

Websites

Coolspotters: The Mega Movie Making Guide For Kids
www.coolspotters.com/articles/the-mega-movie-making-guide-for-kids
This website contains links to a whole raft of great filmmaking resources for young people. Here you can find information on putting together your first storyboard, as well as tips on shooting and editing your first film.

Creative Skillset: Jobs in Film and TV
www.creativeskillset.org/creative_industries/film/job_roles
www.creativeskillset.org/creative_industries/tv/job_roles
If you're interested in working in film or TV one day, this website has loads of great information about different jobs. For example, there is information on well-known roles, such as actor and director. The website also includes details of lesser-known specialist jobs, such as art director, costume designer and agent.

No Film School
www.nofilmschool.com
This is an excellent website for would-be filmmakers. It is designed to help film and TV production enthusiasts learn from one another. Expect step-by-step videos, industry insights and advice on equipment.

Further research

The good news is that, these days, you can find loads of useful information for budding filmmakers on the internet. There are plenty of tutorials on YouTube, and even groups for budding directors on social networks such as Facebook.

Would you like to be taught the basics of filmmaking by professionals? If so, there are loads of companies and organizations that offer taster days and courses for schoolchildren. There may also be a free filmmaking group in your area, where you can exchange ideas, borrow equipment and learn from like-minded people. If you're going to join a group, take a responsible adult along with you.

If you're stuck for ideas, get together with friends or classmates to put together a short film or TV programme for a school project. Alternatively, you could test out your skills by making a film about a school club, group or sports team. If your school has a drama group, you could offer to film their next production. Then, turn it into a DVD for members to keep.

If you need music for your films and TV shows, speak to any musician friends. They might like to create the soundtrack for the piece you're working on. You could even make a music video for the school band, or any friends who have started their own group.

Index